A New Tune

by Charles Broderick
illustrated by Lyle Miller

Core Decodable 93

McGraw Hill Education

Bothell, WA • Chicago, IL • Columbus, OH • New York, NY

MHEonline.com

Copyright © 2015 McGraw-Hill Education

All rights reserved. No part of this publication may be reproduced or distributed in any form or by any means, or stored in a database or retrieval system, without the prior written consent of McGraw-Hill Education, including, but not limited to, network storage or transmission, or broadcast for distance learning.

Send all inquiries to:
McGraw-Hill Education
8787 Orion Place
Columbus, OH 43240

ISBN: 978-0-02-132276-3
MHID: 0-02-132276-7

Printed in the United States of America.

2 3 4 5 6 7 8 9 DOC 20 19 18 17 16 15

Drew played his flute.
He played in his room every day.

Drew played a new tune.
The new tune was very hard.
He did not play it very well.

Drew played and played the tune.
He blew and blew.
Drew had to get it right.

Drew's fingers hurt!
But he still played his flute.
He played every day in June.

It was a very hot summer day.
Flags flew high.
It was time for Drew to play.

Drew had his flute.
Drew played the new tune.
He played the tune very well!